At the end of the day

Alison Bonasoro

BookLeaf
Publishing

India | USA | UK

Made with ❤ on the BookLeaf Publishing Platform
www.bookleafpub.in
www.bookleafpub.com

Dedication

To those who are accepting the nonlinear
journey of healing themselves

Also, to someone who has shown they
genuinely care about a person's well-being

Acknowledgments

I'd like to acknowledge everyone at BookLeaf Publishing for making the publishing dream for writers a reality.

Also, I'd like to acknowledge everyone who supports the writers on their journey.

Preface

This is the third installment of my poetry journey, and I hope all who read it enjoy and maybe even relate.

Learning to stand

When you're born, you don't know how to
stand
You learn to walk, you gain your balance
You take a step or two, and you stumble
You fall if no one is there to hold you up
This is the process
learning how to walk
When I was five, all of a sudden, my knees
gave out on me
It's been like that ever since
I'll be standing, or walking, and then I'm not
Growing up is a lot like that
One day you know how to walk
You can stand with no one holding you up
And then one day
you can be going on your merry way

you'll find yourself stuck in place
knee bent or on the ground
when you can't stand on your own—
no one there to hold you up

Decisions

They say it's good to purge
Every now and again
Decisions, decisions

They say it's best to look at something
Keep it only if it brings you joy
Toss it if it doesn't
Decisions, decisions

They say it's best
Clear space, clear mind
Decisions, decisions

What do you do
When everything means something?
When nothing costs everything
Decisions, decisions

When you get lost in the clutter.
Not only in the clutter of what you're looking
at, but in the decision. Is it joy?
Decisions, decisions

Taking time

Everything hurts, and I want to stay in bed
It's not good to be stuck, so I listen to my
head
I get up and go, but only so-so

I stay awake all night and oversleep during
the day, or not much at all
I know there's one or two shots I tend to no
longer call
I get up and go, but only so-so

What I used to think was strength gained
Through mundane redundancy of
manic-inducing chaos
Is not strength at all
But I get up and go,
Even if it is, only so-so

At the end of the day

Who am I
Who am I if I don't even try
Who am I
Who am I if all I did was talk
Who am I
Who am I at the end of the day
Because at the end of the day
Who I am is all I have

One day

Maybe hopeless
Maybe romantic
Believing in faith
For our one day maybe

Maybe hopeless
Maybe romantic
Maybe I'll never be strong enough
To let myself really know

Maybe hopeless
Maybe romantic
Maybe needing my heart to break;
Maybe our real one day maybe

Autumn and Fall

I don't expect anyone to understand
Sometimes the leaves just fall
No rhyme or reason
The wind just kicks up out of nowhere
Some of the leaves fall while the others hold
on for dear life
We don't know why the ones that fall decided
to let go, if they even had a choice at all
All we know is
We love to jump in colorful piles
We love the sounds underneath our feet
But I don't expect anyone to understand
The fear of letting go

I don't know if I'll end up in a colorful pile
ready to be enjoyed
Or just piled up, ready to be hauled away

The one who pours

If you were to ask me
If the glass is half empty or half full
I bet you're trying to see
If I'm a pessimist or an optimist
I like to think I'm an optimist
But when you've poured out all your love and
never get refilled by another's faucet
It's not so easy to be full or even half full
I've only ever been refilled by the rain of
others' traumas

They come to me for guidance and
reassurance
That feeling of being needed or even wanted
that is what kept my glass filled with any
ounce of water at all
So if you were to ask me
Is the glass half empty or half full
I'll just say, "It's not empty"

Spirals

Just let me spiral
So I can keep going
Just let me overthink
So I know where the underneath of it all is

Just let me spiral
So I can get off the slide
I don't want to reach the top
I need to be settled on the ground
I won't ever ask for the safety net of your
reassurance

Even though knowing it's there will help
It's not your job to catch me or keep me
grounded
I need to be able to do that for myself
Just let me spiral

52

I've never been good at imagination play
Or wanted for team games
Give me a coloring book
A board game
Or even a deck of cards

I've never been good at imagination play
Give me a swing set
A playground
And let me doodle away

I've never been good at imagination play
We can play four-square
Ride our bikes and jump rope
I'll even show you up at skip it
Or we can swim all day

I've never been good at imagination play
Guess I'm not much of a team player
I said you could even give me a deck of cards
But it looks like you have your own deck, and
I'm playing fifty-two pick-up

Again and learning

Here it ignites again,
The flame was in my hands
And for a second
The warmth was hypnotizing
So much so that for the first time in a long
time, my mind went still

So still that I thought,
About how long I could hold this flame;
About how it could burn, even the healthiest
logs into embers.
And for that hypnotizing second when I
could let it burn
I realized I will never truly escape the flame,
but I don't have to let it burn forever

Black isn't on the color wheel

It's the first step out of the front door
It's the shield of armor I wear when I enter
the war
It always has been, and I fear it always will be

I'm learning to walk down these steps
I'm learning to be comfortable without the
armor, eventually not being in the war

It's always been black
But has it always been dark
It's easy to see black
And not the colors that make it
We always see the destination of the door and
not the steps to get there

It's always the war and not the individual
battles or causes
I'm learning to see the colors
And not mix them
To step one at a time
And not jump
To battle the causes one at a time
So I don't have to go to war against them all
at once
There's more than an overall
It's a process, not an outcome

Conducting of my own

It's not something I'm proud of
And it's definitely not a characteristic I wish I
had.
Yet here I am saying this;
I've always been good at finding excuses
Finding excuses and disguising them as
reasons
Of course, there are some things I hold others
accountable for; I was a child when some of
the setbacks took place.

Now I know I surpassed those points, and the
outcomes from those situations are molded by
my own hands.

I can say, "I wish that so and so..." or "if only...
so and so"
But, ultimately, I need to say, "I wish I did
this" or "I have to do this"
I'll always be able to find excuses and
reasons
I can even make up the rhyme to go along.
There's no rhyme or reason from a conductor
anymore.
It's just a beat of my own drum now.

The long game

It's always been an adamant admiration I kept
tucked away for a rainy day.
Call me a hopeless romantic
Because I still tell myself, deep down, you feel
the same way.
We always feel the tether, but the ball never
makes it all the way around the pole.
We keep going back and forth, or we both
walk away.

Guess we're meant to play the long game.
Because it's easier to keep up the rouse.
You know exactly what to say
And I know exactly how to fall.
I say I'm grateful and flattered

And those dull sparks in the absence go full
fireworks.
Yet it's always just talk.
It's just the long game, and I don't know
when to call it game over.

Proud is the goal

I want to make you proud
I hope that I am
I wish I knew if I was
I don't know what it's like observing my
actions
I feel like you'd be yelling at me for some of
my choices and cheering me on for the others
I wish I cared more about making you proud
when you were here
I wish I made better choices for you
We always shuffled the deck because I didn't
know how to play the hand I dealt myself
I wish I could see those choices unfold
Maybe even refold and unfold again
No matter the choices
I hope you and I are proud of both of us

Cat's Cradle

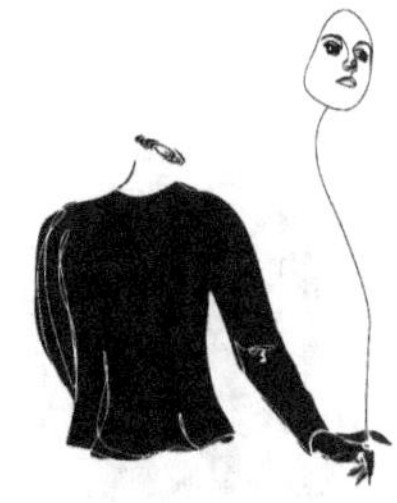

When I come back from our time together
I either feel better about myself
Or I feel worse
There are periods of a string of knots
More of a tangle of matted strings
That I carry around with me
And every so often, they come undone
Until I put it in my boot and walk around
with it
When I get home and take off my boots
I sit with this ball of tangles and knots
Sometimes I just sit and stare
Wonder how this came to be
Other times, I try to undo them
One by one
Knot by knot
Until I realize this is just a cat's cradle

Rest, but don't oversleep

I know there are things I'll never be and
places I'll never see.
I know there are things I wish I never was and
places I never saw.
But both are vital
Both are a part of me
The things I'll never be narrow down what I
am
And the things I was helped with make me
who I am.

I am a hurt person who saw darkness and let
it comfort me like a blanket, and parts of me
thrived in living under the covers.

I think I'm healing
I know if I never snuggled under the covers in
the dark, I would still be there.
I think I am healing, and I know that I know
this because I can no longer comfortably
breathe under the covers.
I'm sure I'll visit my blanket cocoon if I get
hurt again, but I know it will just be a visit.
I'll know when I overslept.
I think I'm healing and can finally tolerate the
light.

Creature

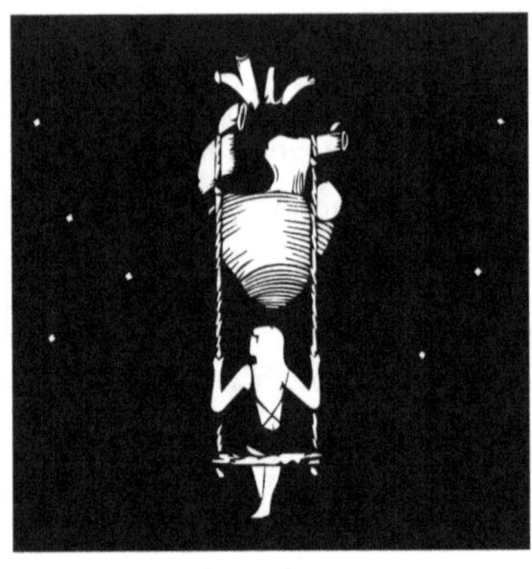

I'm a creature of habit
I'm a creature of comfort
A creature of solitude in my own way
I'm not thrilled with the idea of leaving my
nest
I don't like what it entails
I know what it can do for my evolution
For Mother Nature will ensure it's so
But
I'm a creature of habit
I'm a creature of comfort
A creature of solitude
And I wish I could have it both ways

Crochet history

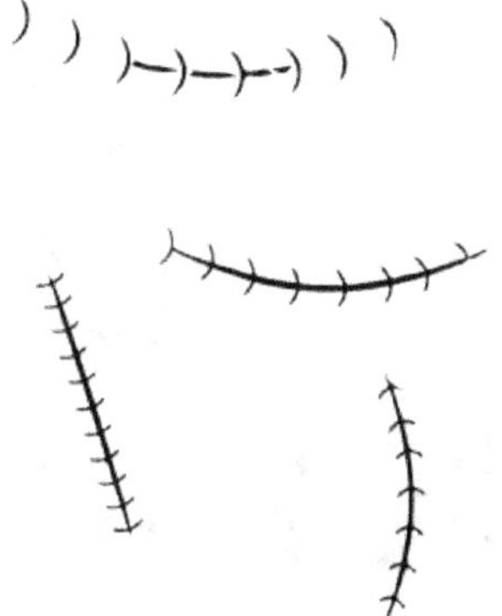

They say history has a way of repeating itself
And everything skips a generation
But when I stop and feel like I'm making a
mistake
And I'm choosing to hit repeat
And relive the choice my parents made for
me back when
Because I grew a lot then
maybe, just maybe
I can crochet a chain of history into one
lifetime

Tell me, help me

Tell me to not give up
Tell me to stop being proud
Tell me it's foolish to have pride
When it comes to needing help

I know it's going to be challenging
But a challenge of pride is a testament to
growth
When taking the easy way out is where your
roots lie

Tell me it's okay to ask for help
Tell me it's okay to give up as long as you
don't make it a habit

Tell me I'm still growing even when
everything falls apart
Because falling apart and rebuilding
Are the only ways you see the growth
But most of all
Tell me you'll be here

The other end

I'm not ashamed to admit
I couldn't commit
That, for the first time, in a long time
I slept with my head
At the other end of my bed
I'm not ashamed of saying
I couldn't go
That when anxiety struck
I could only go home
I'm not ashamed to say
I felt a storm brewing
And for the first time, I couldn't ride it out
I found shelter and,
I slept with my head at the other end of my
bed

One at a time

I don't have the answers
Where do you see yourself?
Where do you want to be?
How do you see yourself?
What do you wish to be?
Where do you wish to be?
The big what?
I don't see anything
I don't feel anything
All I have is a fantasy
I can think up anything and everything
But the reality of it all is I'm not five
The reality of it is

I don't see myself
I never did
And I don't know if I ever will
But I'm here and I can decide
One question at a time